The E Collection

mandy duggan

A catalogue record for this book is available from the National Library of Australia

ISBN: 978-1-922343-90-1

Linellen Press
265 Boomerang Road
Oldbury, Western Australia
www.linellenpress.com.au

Thank you E for being in my life, if only briefly.

Enigma

: a person or thing that is difficult to understand

Love paradox …

Feeling unadulterated joy for your achievements

and

Aching in my heart because you are no longer my lover.

This ache that I feel as I breathe in and out
is not my thoughts creating pain in my body,
it's pain, such that my mind becomes aware of it.

You cannot know the faith and trust that I placed in you.

You cannot know the privilege and honour I bestowed upon you,

by opening my heart and my body to you

simply on an unspoken promise.

I thought you understood how fragile this gift was.

I believed that I was safe with you.

I never told you that I loved you.

As naturally and necessarily as I breathe,

I love you.

I would have danced with you forever

without knowing where I was going.

I thought you would face your fear and your struggle head-on

and let me help you through it.

That the place I held in your heart

and the memory of me

would whisper sweet words of encouragement

in your moments of doubt,

when you stumbled and lost your way.

Whichever way I gaze upon this

I am not so special to you.

This breaks my heart
but I know it's your truth
and I must accept it as such
somehow …

I just hope …

that one day

I can think of you

and not hurt

or that I can

not think of you at all.

I'm so angry at myself

for trusting you.

Even though my adult self knows

this is part of something bigger

and needs to happen for each of us

in exactly this way.

What was I thinking?

Seriously?

Did I really think I could just walk away from you?

Yes I did.

Clearly delusional.

Clearly …

I would really like to talk to you…

like adults

You know …

in the same room,

making eye contact

and being honest.

But then, you know that, right?

That particular night
was so, very, special to me
and always will be
in contrast to what it meant to you.

Is this what you do when you're conflicted?

Withdraw?

Why?

Have you never learned to communicate

and get through the struggle?

The kindest thing you could do for me right now

would be to communicate with me.

I also think this is the kindest thing you could do for yourself.

I see something beautiful

and I want to share it with you;

it is really that simple.

I can't imagine

that you don't want to share things with me anymore.

You talked to me about the things

we would do together

and we couldn't stop smiling at each other.

Then you wouldn't speak to me.

Embers

: small pieces of glowing coal or wood in a dying fire

I go for days without thinking of you,

then a memory fills my mind

so vividly that it feels real,

before I realise you're not here

and the loss and the ache start all over again.

Secretly…

in the part of me that no-one sees,

I hope with all my might

that we will be together again.

shhhh… don't tell.

I long to hear your voice

the sound of your laughter

and to feel how that moves over my skin,

cocooning me.

I don't want to let go of the memories of us,

I play them in my mind,

my favourite love story,

over and over again.

Self-torture.

Letting go …

is my new mantra,

over and over,

as many times as I think of you

I say it.

Letting go … Letting go … Letting go …

is how I am trying to condition my brain

to replace memories of you.

I'm not sure it's working.

You say that we are friends

yet I'm not sure that is so.

Friends chat regularly and catch up over coffee.

You don't communicate with me at all.

If I message you, you don't reply.

That is not how you treat a friend.

I'm on an emotional rollercoaster.

I reach the point that I want to communicate with you.

I miss you and I want to ask how you are

and then I crash into this sadness and loneliness

and wish I hadn't messaged you.

Am I in denial?

Am I hanging onto what I wish could be?

Or are my feelings real?

Am I hanging on because I cannot let go?

It is not easy to stop being your lover

and be your friend.

I cannot be your friend

while I want to be your lover.

I want to be your lover,

I am not your friend.

I wanted to reach out to you this morning,

to hear your voice,

connect with you.

So badly …

While my heart and my mind are in conflict

my soul speaks the truth.

Did I really love you?

Perhaps I loved the reflection of myself

that I found in you.

My memories of you
have faded with time.
Yet I remember how I felt
When I was with you.

I find myself staring into space,
thinking of the way your eyes smiled
when you looked at me.
One of my favourite memories.

I am letting go now,

those lingering threads are wearing thin.

Soon I will no longer feel your cheek against the wall.

Do you think of me?

Do you have memories of your time with me

that you wrap carefully and keep safe?

Do you feel my cheek against the wall?

Engender

: cause or give rise to (a feeling, situation or condition)

Synonyms: cause, be the cause of, give rise to, bring about, lead to, result in, produce, create, generate, arouse, rouse, provoke, incite, kindle, trigger, spark off, touch off, stir up, whip up, induce, inspire, instigate, foment, effect, occasion, promote, foster; *literary* beget, enkindle; *Rare* effectuate

When we were travelling together in a taxi,

I asked you to make something happen.

I implored you to act before it was too late,

you kissed me goodnight!

Neither of us could have known that kiss would rock our world,

that one kiss would connect us for years,

transcend us into a fantasy of reliving and longing for more.

Yet, I wonder if this would have happened

if I had not asked you to act before it was too late.

I thought of you often in those years.

It infuriated me as much as it fed my fantasy

that we couldn't be together.

Yet our connection was so strong.

I tried so hard to let you go,
to let go of the fantasy,
to get on with my life,
to let go.
I failed dismally.

Would you have held on for so long

if not for my constant messaging?

If not for my sharing my thoughts with you?

If not for my actions, would I just be a faded memory for you?

I was at the brink of letting go
eight years on,
when I shared *the Dance* with you
and you asked me to take your hand.
Would you have asked me to dance
had I not shared that prose with you?

Did I manifest our relationship
when you were not ready?
Or did you truly think you were ready
and then realise that you weren't?

My continual reaching out to you,
is this me keeping something alive
that should have died on 19 February?

I feel you on the other side of the wall that you put up between us.

Your cheek against the wall, your arm above your head.

Your tears, your frustration.

I can hear your breathing, your pain.

Just that metaphorical wall between us

and this gaping void.

I observed you closely when we were together,

to be sure that you wanted to be in that moment.

I noticed you reach for my hand and wrap yours around it.

You impulsively kiss me in public.

You touch my body out of your own need.

These were actions that I did not cause.

They were yours, your choice.

I am certain of it.

Now I have no causal effect on you,

every communication I make with you

is met with silence that causes me such heartache.

Or is your silence, the result of causal effect?

I can no longer remember how your voice sounds

or feel the vibration of your sound,

the smell of you, or how your skin feels.

Yet I can still feel your cheek against the wall.

If I were to stop contacting you,

to completely remove myself from your life

would you even remember who I am?

Would I never hear from you again?

Gone from your life forever?

This certainty that I have
that we care deeply about each other
is unwavering.
Even though it makes no sense.

My head tells me to forget you,

my heart tells me to hold on.

My soul sits beside yours in complete serenity.

I find myself in a position of powerlessness,

not able to cause *me* to be in *your* life,

beyond knowing that you read my messages.

So I focus on causing *you* to be in *my* life

even if it's not real.

I've been able to give up

cigarettes, alcohol and caffeine,

a toxic marriage,

but I haven't been able to give up on you.

I really want you to be the one

to close this gap between us.

I need to know you want to be with me,

not because I did something to cause this to happen

but because you did something to cause this to happen.

About the Author

Mandy Duggan is a published author, blogger and songwriter who lives in the south west of Western Australia. Retirement in 2015 due to a chronic health condition was life-changing and Mandy wrote her first book as a powerful healing tool for herself and readers. Mandy felt compelled to share her own story; if her journey could help just one person then it made it worthwhile. Becoming a published author has also created the opportunity for Mandy to give inspirational talks which have been an amazing experience.

Lightning Source UK Ltd.
Milton Keynes UK
UKHW020509240621
386027UK00002B/19